Rise of the Thinking
MACHINES
The Science of ROBOTS

HEADLINE SCIENCE

Robots···Headline Science···Robots···Headline Science

by Jennifer Fretland VanVoorst

Content Adviser:
Trey Smith, Ph.D., Systems Scientist,
Carnegie Mellon University West/
NASA Ames Intelligent Robotics Group

Science Adviser:
Terrence E. Young Jr., M.Ed., M.L.S.,
Jefferson Parish (Louisiana) Public School System

Reading Adviser:
Rosemary G. Palmer, Ph.D., Department of Literacy,
College of Education, Boise State University

Compass Point Books • 151 Good Counsel Drive, P. O. Box 669 • Mankato, MN 56002-0669

This book was manufactured with paper containing
at least 10 percent post-consumer waste.

Library of Congress Cataloging-in-Publication Data
VanVoorst, Jennifer Fretland, 1972–
  Rise of the thinking machines: the science of robots / By Jennifer Fretland VanVoorst.
     p. cm.—(Headline Science)
  Includes index.
  ISBN 978-0-7565-3377-9 (library binding)
  ISBN 978-0-7565-3518-6 (paperback)
1. Robots—Juvenile literature. I. Title. II. Series.
  TJ211.V35 2008
  629.8'92—dc22   2008005732

Editor: Anthony Wacholtz
Designers: Ellen Schofield and Ashlee Suker
Page Production: Bobbie Nuytten
Photo Researcher: Eric Gohl

Art Director: LuAnn Ascheman-Adams
Creative Director: Keith Griffin
Editorial Director: Nick Healy
Managing Editor: Catherine Neitge

Photographs ©: Malte Christians/Bongarts/Getty Images, cover (bottom), 35; Tate Carlson/iStock-
photo, cover (inset, left), 12; DARPA, cover (inset, middle), 28; NASA/JPL-Caltech, cover (inset, right),
33; Press Association via AP Images, 5; AP Images/*Columbus Dispatch*, Shari Lewis, 7; AP Images/
Shizuo Kambayashi, 8; Yoshikazu Tsuno/AFP/Getty Images, 9, 20, 23; AP Images/Mike Derer, 11, 24;
Baloncici/Shutterstock, 13; Horizon/Art Life Images, 14; Plus Pix/Art Life Images, 15; AP Images/
Katsumi Kasahara, 16, 43; Alex Wong/Getty Images, 18; AP Images/*The Morning Call*, Cesar L. Laure,
19; AP Images/Reed Saxon, 21; Koichi Kamoshida/Getty Images, 22; AP Images/Robert F. Bukaty, 25;
AP Images/Kyodo, 27; Paolo Patrizi/Alamy, 29, 37; Velodyne Lidar, Inc., 30; Douglas McFadd/Getty
Images, 31; NASA/Getty Images, 32; AP Images/The RoboCup Federation, HO, 34; Sam Ogden/Photo
Researchers, Inc., 39; Rick Friedman/Corbis, 40; AP Images/Koji Ueda, 41; Globe Photos, 42.

Visit Compass Point Books on the Internet at *www.compasspointbooks.com*
or e-mail your request to *custserv@compasspointbooks.com*

ROBOTS: THE FUTURE IS NOW

>>> CNN.com
April 18, 2006

Humans have always been fascinated by the idea of robots. Science-fiction, so often the medium through which society explores the potential impact of new technology, has always been obsessed with robots, and some of the most enduring sci-fi characters have been robots, from R2D2 and C3PO, to The Terminator and Data.

But robots are already a part of our lives. Industrial robots (are) widely used in manufacturing. Military and police organizations use robots to assist in dangerous situations. Robots can be found exploring the surface of Mars, and vacuuming the floors in your home.

Robots are all around us. When most people think of a robot, they think of a machine built in the image of a person. In reality, most robots don't look anything like us. They are Mars rovers, deep-sea explorers, or mechanical arms that assemble car bodies on a factory floor. In fact, robots may even be in your home right now. You may have a robotic vacuum cleaner vacuuming your floor or a robotic lawn mower trimming the grass.

Most robots are designed to perform specific tasks. Because of this, robots can be very different from each other. Pioneering roboticist Joseph

In March 2008, Husqvarna—an outdoor power equipment company—released the Automower Solar Hybrid, a self-powered lawn mower that runs on solar energy and electricity.

KEEPING CURRENT

News changes every minute, and readers need access to the latest information to keep current. Here are a few key search terms to help you locate up-to-the-minute robots headlines:

artificial intelligence (AI)

Center for Robot-Assisted
   Search and Rescue
   (CRASAR)

DARPA Urban Challenge

nanorobots

Predator drone

RoboCup

robot-assisted surgery

robot code of ethics

Engelberger once said, "I can't define a robot, but I know one when I see one." One thing all robots have in common is a movable body that can perform some kind of action. The action may be walking, rolling, or flying. It can also be the ability to interact with the world through a grasping hand or a lifting arm. Sometimes this action is preprogrammed into the robot. Other times the action is remote-controlled by a human. The action can even be a decision made by the robot itself.

WHY BUILD ROBOTS?

The word *robot* was first used in the 1921 play *R.U.R.* (*Rossum's Universal Robots*) by the Czech writer Karel Capek. The term comes from the Czech word *robota,* which means "forced labor." In Capek's play, an inventor and his son create robots for factory work. Today's robots are built to work in factories and to perform other tasks as well—tasks that are too dull, difficult, or dangerous for people to do.

Robots are well-suited for tasks many humans find dull. Robots are good for these jobs because they will work long hours, do not need to be paid, and do not have something else they would rather do.

We also build robots to do work that is difficult for humans to do. Robots can lift more and make more precise movements than a human. They can perform these tasks over and over again, exactly the same way each time.

Robots can do work that a human cannot do safely. They go into space, under water, or into toxic waste dumps. There are robots that defuse bombs and tiny robots that explore places we cannot travel.

WHAT ROBOTS LOOK LIKE

Because robots are built for different tasks, they don't look the same. Some

A robot used by the Columbus Division of Fire Bomb Squad raises a car onto two of its tires during a demonstration in Ohio.

robots look like animals. For example, six-legged robots can easily scramble up rocks just like an insect does. Snakelike robots can explore narrow passages. Some robots are built like fish so they can swim. Other robots are built like humans so they can move about our homes and offices. Some can even walk up stairs. Some robots have hands to grasp things, while others have arms so they can move things. Nature has given us ideas about how to build robots for various purposes. This is called biomimicry—making a robot that looks and moves like a living thing.

THREE KINDS OF ROBOTS

Robotics—the study of robots—is a very broad field. Because robots are so

A robotic coelacanth—an ancient fish—was on display at the Mitsubishi Minatomirai Industrial Museum in Yokohama, Japan. The robotic fish is 32 inches (80 centimeters) long and weighs 27 pounds (12 kilograms).

different from one another, they are sometimes grouped into three classifications. The three divisions are based on how the robot performs an action.

Programmed robots perform their actions over and over under the control of a computer. Teleoperated robots are operated by humans using remote control. Autonomous robots use sensors to learn about their world, and then they use an onboard computer to "think" about the action they should take. These three types of robots have different abilities that set them apart from one another.

ASIMO

Humanoid robots—robots with a human form—have advantages over other kinds of robots when it comes to operating in a world built for people. One of the most advanced humanoid robots is ASIMO, which stands for "Advanced Step in Innovative Mobility." It is the 11th generation of robots that Honda created to walk like humans. One of the most recent advances is ASIMO's ability to walk up and down stairs. Robots that have wheels usually can't climb stairs. ASIMO can also run, grasp objects, and recognize gestures. ASIMO can understand and respond to simple voice commands. It can also recognize faces and address those people by name. Someday humanoid robots like ASIMO might help with important tasks such as assisting the elderly or people who use wheelchairs.

NEED MORE WORKERS? TRY A ROBOT

CNN Money
September 24, 2007

Two of the best workers at Blue Chip, a manufacturing shop in Columbus [Ohio], don't take lunch breaks. These model employees draw no salary, work unlimited shifts, and weld at lightning speed. Their performance isn't just superhuman—it isn't human at all. "My robots are wonderful," says Steve Tatman, vice president of engineering at Blue Chip. ... "Since adding them to the team, we've become more competitive and more efficient." ...

Industrial robots have long been commonplace in large manufacturing operations such as auto plants. Today some 171,000 robots toil in North American factories, and sales jumped 39% in the first half of 2007, according to the Robotics Industries Association.

Industrial and manufacturing robots use programs to complete a task. A program is a set of instructions used by a computer, and programmed robots use a computer to carry out their actions. These programs are more commonly called software. Programmed robots perform the same actions time after time. So what makes them different from dishwashers, washing machines, or any of the other mechanical devices you have around your house? Robots are reprogrammable. The computer inside the robot can accept a new set of instructions. For example, the robot might be programmed to pack boxes. The robot can be reprogrammed the next day to move those same boxes. Dishwashers, however, cannot be programmed to perform different tasks. A dishwasher can only wash dishes.

TAKING ACTION

When you take action, you use muscles to move your arms, head, and feet. While the human body has muscles, robots have actuators—

Engineering students from Monmouth University in New Jersey programmed robots to push balls into the pockets of a pool table.

devices that cause action to take place. Examples of actuators include motors and hydraulic systems that operate hands, arms, wheels, and treads. Anything on the robot that can be commanded to move is an actuator.

The difference between the three classifications of robots is how the action is decided upon. In a programmed robot, the action is a repeated script determined by the instructions programmed into the robot's computer.

MANUFACTURING OUR WORLD

The biggest use of robots right now is in manufacturing. Robots have been used in industry and manufacturing since 1961, when the first industrial robot was installed at a General Motors factory. This 4,000-pound (1,800-kg) robotic arm, called the

Unimate, stacked sheets of hot metal. Today there are more than 1 million industrial robots in use worldwide. They work for weeks, months, or even

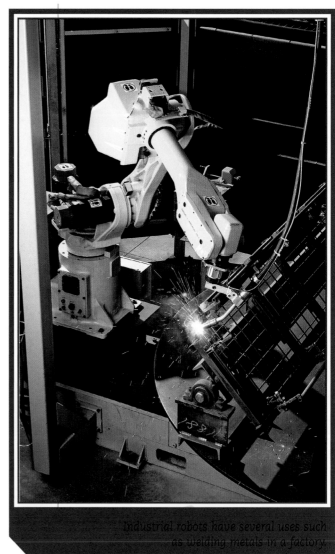

Industrial robots have several uses such as welding metals in a factory.

years lifting, loading, packing, or painting. The robots repeat these actions until they are programmed to do something else.

Industrial robots are used to do jobs that require a high degree of accuracy. These robots can be more accurate than people because they can do things exactly the same way every time. They don't make mistakes

NOW YOU KNOW

Of the more than 1 million industrial robots in use worldwide, more than half are installed in factories in Asia. Japan has more robots than any other nation.

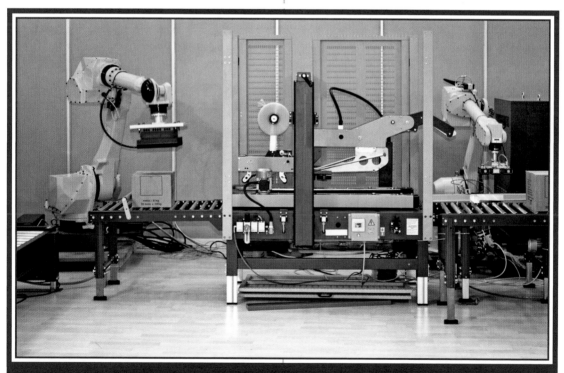

Work done on an assembly line can be completed faster by using multiple robots, each with its own function.

because they don't get tired, bored, or distracted. They also can work for long periods at a time without a break, and they don't run the risk of injury from heavy lifting or repetitive strain. Still, robots require maintenance and sometimes need to be replaced.

One of the biggest users of industrial robots is the automobile industry. Roughly half of the world's automobile industry's labor force is made up of robots. Robots are well-suited to assembly-line work. Since robots are designed based on the tasks they need to perform, most industrial robots are simply multijointed arms on a stand or movable platform. These arms, called manipulators, are controlled by

Using robotic arms in an assembly line has made automobile factories more efficient and much safer for human workers.

a computer. They can be programmed to perform the same task over and over. They can also be used to do dangerous tasks such as welding, gluing, painting, and assembling car bodies.

PROGRAMMING THE ROBOT

To complete a task, a programmed robot follows specific instructions. For example, an industrial robot that takes a car door off of a conveyor belt is told how far to reach its arm, how tightly to grasp the door, and where to put it down. This information is programmed into the robot's memory.

The robot has an internal computer that a human can program in a variety of ways. One way is by creating step-by-step instructions using a computer programming language. These instructions might be:

1. Turn 10 degrees to the left.
2. Bend elbow 40 degrees down.
3. Wait 2 seconds.
4. Close hand.
5. Bend elbow up 40 degrees.
6. Turn 10 degrees to the right.
7. Release hand.
8. Return to step 1 and repeat sequence.

HEADLINE SCIENCE

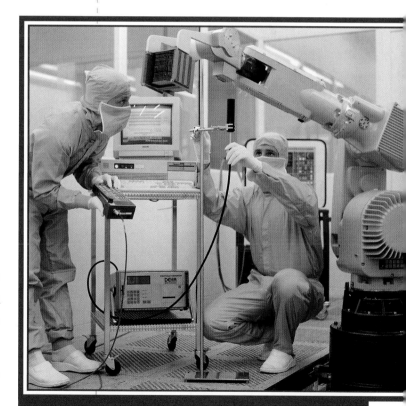

A robotic arm helped engineers handle delicate equipment inside a "clean room."

While the actual program for a robot may be detailed instructions, the methods people use to create these programs can be very simple. Some robots are programmed by example; a human operator physically guides the robot through each step. The robot remembers the motion to use later.

An operator can also program robots by pointing and clicking on computer diagrams with a mouse. For example, suppose a robot needs to weld two pieces of metal together for a car. The operator might load the design of the car into a computer program and then click on the parts to be welded. The robot's computer translates this information into a detailed list of actions. No matter how the robot's program is created, in the end it is simply a step-by-step set of instructions for the robot to follow.

The robot might do its programmed task thousands of times a day. But because it is reprogrammable, it may be programmed to perform a different series of tasks the next day. By keeping a collection of programs ready to load into the robot, an operator can quickly change the robot's tasks from one day to another.

The robot Robovie-M was created by Vstone. Owners assemble and program the robot themselves.

NEW VIDEOS SHOW PREDATORS AT WORK IN IRAQ

>>> CNN.com
February 9, 2005

[M]ilitary video reveals unmanned U.S. Predators firing Hellfire missiles to rescue U.S. troops under fire in Iraq and destroy insurgent targets. ... The video came from sensors on Air Force Predator unmanned aerial vehicles, which can operate several miles away from positions they target and monitor. ...

Pilots more than 7,000 miles away in Nevada control the unmanned planes from their post at Nellis Air Force Base. Their sophisticated cockpits resemble a high-priced video game. Predator crews, which have a pilot and sensor operator, run the craft 24 hours, rotating in three-hour shifts. Predator teams are trained to look for signs of insurgent activity such as the planting of roadside bombs.

Another type of robot is teleoperated robots, or telerobots. "Teleoperated" means remote controlled, or controlled at a distance. There are fewer teleoperated robots than programmed robots, but telerobots are more complex and do more interesting and varied tasks. These robots serve as stand-ins for people in places that are too dangerous or difficult for people to go. Teleoperated robots have explored the interior of active volcanoes, defused bombs in war zones, and even explored the sunken wreckage of the *Titanic*. They have been sent into deep space, toxic waste dumps, and even inside human bodies.

An officer for the Metro Explosive Ordnance Disposal Unit in Washington, D.C., operated a 500-pound (225-kg) robot used to safely disarm bombs. Because of the robot's treaded tires, the officer can move it over rough terrain.

SENSING AND ACTING

Teleoperated robots do not perform preprogrammed actions like programmed robots do. Instead, they act out commands from human controllers, who are sometimes many miles away. Teleoperated robots allow us to overcome our physical limitations while still allowing us to act as if we were there.

To take action, we have to know what is around us. Humans have five senses that allow us to experience the world. Similarly, teleoperated robots carry sensors, electronic equipment that gathers information on the robot's environment. A video camera is a common sensor a robot might carry. The video feed is sent back to the human controller, who sees from

Teleoperated robots roamed the hallways at Harrison Morton Middle School in Allentown, Pennsylvania. Students navigated the robots using computers in a classroom.

the perspective of the robot. The human thinks about what the robot should do and then, using joysticks or other controllers, makes the robot take action.

There are a few kinds of actions a telerobot will normally do. One is motion, which can come in many forms—from flying to walking to rolling—depending on how the robot is built. The operator steers the robot where the robot needs to go to do its job. Teleoperated robots can also interact with the world. This may mean picking something up with a robotic hand, cutting a wire, or operating a

An engineer demonstrated the abilities of a teleoperated TMSUK robot during a 2007 press conference in Tokyo, Japan.

A team of students directed their robot to pick up a large ball during a For Inspiration and Recognition of Science and Technology (FIRST) competition in Los Angeles.

fire extinguisher. This action is usually tied to the kind of mission for which the robot was created. Finally, the robot can simply "look around." This is accomplished by the human operator changing where the robot's sensors are pointing.

SEARCH AND RESCUE

One recent use of telerobots is search and rescue. The first known use of robots for this purpose was after the September 11, 2001, attacks on the World Trade Center. Robotics expert Robin Murphy heads the Center for Robot-Assisted Search and Rescue at the University of South Florida. She and three graduate students drove 18 hours to New York City to search the rubble for victims.

Eight tiny, treaded robots were connected to their human operator by cables. These cables electronically relayed data from the robot to the human. They also transmitted instruc- tions from the human to the robot. The robots were equipped with a variety of sensors. These sensors included microphones that listened for voices, infrared sensors that detected body heat, and cameras that searched for colors among the gray dust that blanketed the site. They were also equipped with night-vision cameras,

Soryu, a search and rescue robot made by Kawasaki Robotics in Japan, is able to move through debris. It uses a color-video camera to locate trapped victims.

The robot ACM-R5 from the Tokyo Institute of Technology is a small-scale search-and-rescue robot that moves from side to side like a snake. The robot can even glide across water.

of structural collapse. Because of their small size, they could get into spaces that people and rescue dogs could not. They could also go much deeper into the rubble to find remains than conventional search equipment. The robots ventured as far as 30 feet (10 meters) into the rubble. Traditional cameras attached to poles could only see in about 7 feet (2 m).

INTO THE BODY

Human beings also use telerobots in the field of medicine to work inside the human body. Robot-assisted surgery gives surgeons greater precision and control. Surgeons do not have to be in the same room—or even in the same city—as the patient they are operating on.

allowing the rescuers to see deep into the rubble where there was little or no light. They could enter places that were still on fire or that posed a risk

In telerobotic surgery, the surgeon sits at a console that displays 3-D images of the inside of the patient's body. These images are transmitted by a camera that has been inserted into the patient's body using a small tube. The surgeon uses joysticks to control robotic arms that sit on a cart beside the patient. These arms are equipped with surgical instruments. As the surgeon moves the controls, the robot translates those movements into commands. It then executes those commands by making the same surgical movements inside the patient's body.

Robot-assisted surgery has many

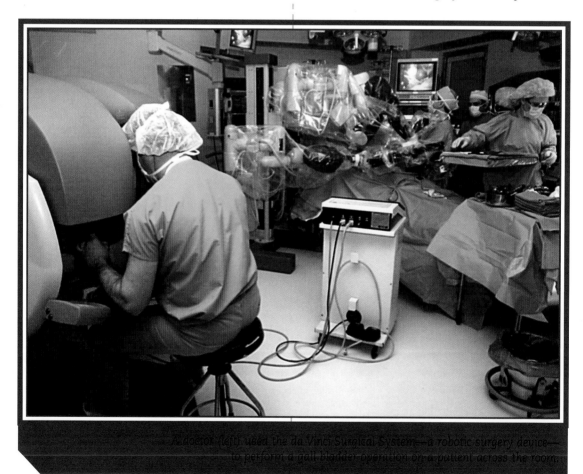

A doctor (left) used the da Vinci Surgical System—a robotic surgery device—to perform a gall bladder operation on a patient across the room.

advantages. The equipment can miniaturize motion so that a large movement by the surgeon becomes a small movement by the robot. This results in smaller, more precise movements. The robot can also filter out hand tremors that can be dangerous during operations. Research shows that patients operated on by teleoperated robots lose less blood during surgery and have

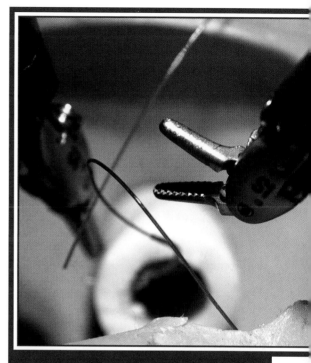

The tiny hands of a surgical robot are used for medical procedures that require detailed movements, such as stitching.

NOW YOU KNOW

Nanotechnology is a field in which scientists are working to create materials on a scale of 1 billionth of a meter. They are working on using nanotechnology to make nanomachines. They believe it may be possible someday to make microscopic robots called "nanobots." Nanobots could flow in your bloodstream and be used by doctors to help heal organs from the inside.

quicker recovery times. Telerobotic surgery also gives people living in remote areas the opportunity to be operated on by an expert surgeon, regardless of the surgeon's location. According to roboticist Ron Arkin, "I have said on the record that, God forbid, I should need hip replacement surgery, I'd rather have a robot do it."

NO DRIVER, NO PROBLEM AS ROBOT CARS FINISH RACE

>> Reuters
November 3, 2007

Cars sprouting whirling lasers on top, moving cameras on the sides, and banks of computers inside sped through the streets of a California desert ghost town on Saturday in a robot race—no drivers needed.

Encouraging future scientists is part of the goal of the robot car race, the latest U.S. Defense Department challenge to universities, companies and inventors. ... The cars run completely by computer, without human intervention, using sensors to plot and pick their way.

Saturday's Urban Challenge sent them along neighborhood roads, through traffic and around jams created by humans. ... The most spectacular error was a minor fender bender which did not stop or significantly damage either vehicle.

Most people who think of robots think of smart robots that do things on their own, not robots that are preprogrammed or under remote control. These robots are called autonomous robots.

THE SENSE-THINK-ACT CYCLE

Programmed robots are programmed to take action. Teleoperated robots carry sensors. But an autonomous robot has sensors and is programmed to look at the data its sensors gather to determine its own actions. In robotics, this is called the "sense-think-act" cycle. The robot takes in sensor data, analyzes what the sensor data mean, and decides on an action. For human beings, interpreting information gathered by our senses is the job of the brain, and it takes place

TPR-Robina is a tour guide robot created by Toyota Motor Corporation. The robot—which has autonomous moving capabilities and can interact with people—escorted visitors through the Toyota Kaikan Exhibition Hall in Nagoya, Japan.

without any effort. For autonomous robots, this work is done by a computer. Software is used to coordinate all the sensor input signals, develop a plan of action, and issue commands to the robotic actuators.

A robot's sensory system must operate much like a human's. Most people use the sense of sight as the main way to perceive the world. If you close your eyes and try to walk into the next room and pick up a

ROBOTS WITH REFLEXES

Human beings have behaviors called reflexes. Our reflexes protect us by getting us out of harm quickly. If you put your hand on a hot stove, for example, you don't waste time deciding that you don't want to burn your hand and determining the best method for removing it. You just pull it away.

Robots can have these kinds of reflexes as well. Autonomous robots are sometimes programmed to respond in specific ways to certain sensor input. For example, some of the autonomous vehicles in the Urban Challenge were programmed to slam on the brakes if they sensed they were

about to hit something. They bypassed the thinking stage of the sense-think-act cycle to react reflexively. By allowing autonomous robots to act without thinking in emergency situations, scientists help keep their robots safe.

HEADLINE SCIENCE

book, you will probably hit the wall or pick up the wrong book. The same is true for a robot. Knowing where things are in the world is important so the robot can do its task. Therefore, the sensors that robots use often focus on seeing.

While video cameras are a good sensor for humans to use when remote controlling a robot, there are other sensors a robot might use when trying to "see" the world for itself. Some robots use a pair of cameras, which gives the robot depth perception so it can determine the distance between itself and the objects it sees. Another way robots determine distance is by using a laser. Light from a laser travels at the speed of light—about 186,000 miles (300,000 kilometers) per second. By timing how long it takes for the light to reflect back, the

A team of robots that interact with one another is used to patrol a mall in Japan. The robots can operate elevators, identify employees, and send video footage to the main security room. Their sensors can also detect humans, fires, and water leaks.

robot can tell how far away an object is that the laser beam hit. By scanning this laser back and forth, and then up and down, the robot can make a three-dimensional map of nearby objects. This type of scanning laser is called a lidar.

The same approach can also be done using sound waves. This is called sonar. If the robot uses radio waves, it is called radar. Each approach has advantages and disadvantages. For example, a lidar may give very accurate distance information, but it offers no information about the color of the object the laser bounced off of. By combining different sources of sensor information, the robot can gain more information about the world around it. This is called sensor fusion.

Velodyne's lidar sensor collects 1.8 million data points per second to create a 360-degree, three-dimensional map of its surroundings.

Because robots are built in different ways for different purposes, it makes sense that they are programmed to "think" in different ways, too. The programs an autonomous robot uses to interpret sensor data and take action can be very simple or very complex, depending on what the robot is designed to do. For example, the Roomba, a robotic vacuum cleaner, has simple programming. It heads in one direction, and when it detects an obstacle, it picks a new direction and starts over. By doing this over and over, there is a good chance that it will eventually vacuum the entire room.

The Urban Challenge robotic vehicles that drive in traffic feature much more sophisticated "thinking." These vehicles keep track of their locations and the locations of other cars, both of which are continually changing. They also pay attention to traffic laws. When they come to an intersection, they keep track of what cars are already there and wait their turn, based on the rules of the road.

The robot manufacturer iRobot created the Roomba—an automatic vacuum cleaner.

EXPLORING SPACE

In January 2004, two robots—*Spirit* and *Opportunity*—touched down on Martian soil. Their mission was to look for signs that Mars once had water. If the planet had water—and for a long enough time—it might have once sustained life.

Known as rovers, *Spirit* and *Opportunity* are autonomous robots. Although they can communicate with mission control on Earth using a high-powered antenna, the time lag between Earth and Mars is too long to allow for teleoperation. Therefore, the robots are programmed with missions and are left on their own to complete them.

During a typical day, each rover sends image, instrument, and status data to Earth. Scientists make decisions based on that data. For example,

NASA technicians at the Kennedy Space Center in Florida tested a Mars exploration rover before it was sent into space.

they can look at the images the rover sends back and identify a rock in the distance that they would like it to investigate. They send instructions to the robot to drive over to that rock and gather data using one of its six onboard scientific instruments. The scientists send their commands to the rover during a three-hour window of direct communication with the high-powered antenna. The rover is then on its own for 20 hours, carrying out its commands.

Even though the robots have received a set of instructions, they still sense, think, and act to carry them out. The rovers sense their environment using three pairs of navigation cameras on the front, back, and mast of the rover. These cameras let the robot "see" its surroundings. Its computer then gathers the information received by the cameras to build a map of its surroundings. It identifies any obstacles that may lie in its path. If the robot can't find safe passage to the rock it is supposed to study, the robot will plan a new path that avoids the obstacles. Six motorized wheels and a manipulator arm allow the robot to carry out its mission.

One of the rovers' missions was to learn about the history of water on Mars.

WORKING AS A TEAM

Robots that work by themselves are just beginning to be developed. Many competitions have been organized to give robot researchers goals to focus on. One such competition is RoboCup, in which two teams of autonomous robots face off in a game of soccer. The goal of this competition is to have a team of autonomous soccer-playing robots that, by 2050, can beat the world's best human team. The Robo-

NOW YOU KNOW

Many schools around the world have a robotics competition in which the robots are made of Legos. Teams of students use a specific set of Lego pieces from the "Mindstorm" Lego kit to create an autonomous robot with actuators and sensors.

Autonomous robotic dogs lined up for a play during a RoboCup match.

Cup competition is held each year, with several hundred teams from more than 30 countries. At the first RoboCup in 1997, the robots could barely find the ball or make progress toward moving it. Today the robots are much more sophisticated. While RoboCup roboticists have a long way to go before their robots can beat the best human players, these robots are excellent examples of autonomous robots that sense, think, and act.

The robots in the RoboCup tournaments learn to block, kick, and pass the ball from past experience.

Many teams have given their soccer-playing robots three "behaviors": attack, defend, and intercept. The robots use their sensors and decide which behavior they should use. The robot players must sense the ball, their teammates, their opponents, the goal, and their position on the field.

To sense the ball, for example, most robots use cameras. They try to recognize the ball by its unique color. Once they sense the ball and its position, they analyze what would be the best move. Then they translate the data into physical action on the field. For example, if they sense that they are in possession of the ball, then they perform their "attack" by lining up the ball with the goal and dribbling the ball over to the goal. If they sense that the other team is in possession of the ball, they either attempt to intercept the ball or retreat to their goal to help block.

PUBLIC MEETING WILL RE-EXAMINE FUTURE OF ARTIFICIAL INTELLIGENCE

>>> *San Francisco Chronicle*
September 7, 2007

For decades, scientists and writers have imagined a future with walking, talking robots that could do everything from cooking your eggs to enslaving your planet. Trouble is, this fabled artificial intelligence has never happened.

But this weekend, more than 700 scientists and tech industry leaders will gather at San Francisco's Palace of Fine Arts Theatre to plan for the day ... when computers start improving themselves without the approval of their former masters. ...

[A] growing number of computer scientists, ethicists, industrialists, and forward-thinkers believe that, far from improbable, machine intelligence seems to be evolving.

Right now, robots are being developed and used for specific purposes, but the most exciting goal of roboticists is to create a robot that has the intellectual capability of a human being. This requires a robot to know all the things that a human being knows. But how can that be accomplished? That challenge falls to a field of computer science called artificial intelligence (AI). This area of research works to dramatically increase the "thinking" component of the sense-think-act cycle.

ARTIFICIAL INTELLIGENCE

Scientists who work in AI try to recreate the power of the human brain.

Kotaro, a humanoid robot from the University of Tokyo in Japan, has 120 actuators designed for future robotic technologies. One of the robotics professors at the university stated Kotaro is the first step in creating service robots that will one day be in individual homes.

They attempt to create a robot that can "think" like us—that can learn, reason, use language, develop original ideas, and do all the other things the human brain can do. In 1950, computer scientist Alan Turing devised a method he called an "imitation game" for determining a machine's intelligence. According to Turing, a machine is artificially intelligent if a person interacting with it (but who can't see it) thinks he or she is interacting with a human being. The "Turing Test" is still a common way to determine AI.

There are two views about artificial intelligence. One belief suggests that to make a machine artificially intelligent, it must be programmed to know all the things a human being knows. This is called the "top-down" approach.

But programming a computer to contain all the knowledge of a typical human brain is an overwhelming task. It may not even be possible. Therefore, researchers today typically practice a "bottom-up" approach, in which robots have the ability to learn in a limited capacity. Learning robots can

NOW YOU KNOW

Some scientists predict that with the current trends in computer technology, computers can become artificially intelligent by 2030. Since computer processing power doubles approximately every 18 months, computers could be twice as smart as humans in 2032, four times as smart in 2034, and eight times as smart in 2036.

recognize if a certain action achieves a desired result.

For example, dribbling the ball is a difficult task for robots in the RoboCup competition. Members of a team from the University of Texas have developed a training exercise by which their robot practices moving the ball for hours. Each time, the robot performs its movements a little differently and watches to see the effect on ball control. Movements that lead to more control are remembered as good, and movements that lead to less control are remembered as bad. By practicing more ways of making good movements, the robot learns the best method of dribbling the ball.

One supporter of the bottom-up view of AI is Cynthia Breazeal, the director of the Massachusetts Institute of Technology's Robotic Life Group. Her latest creation, a furry autonomous robot named Leonardo, is designed to interact socially.

The autonomous robot Leonardo was named after the famous Italian artist and scientist Leonardo da Vinci.

HEADLINE SCIENCE

Leonardo learns by interacting with human users. It has a variety of facial expressions and can use them appropriately. It can also grab objects and make complex gestures. Leonardo can even learn simple tasks such as turning lights on and off. Leonardo learns how to complete a task by direct instruction or by imitating the actions of a human performing the task. It can also learn by observing a human's reaction to performing a task. Breazeal says,

> I'm interested in building robots that can learn ... in the human environment (like my own kids!). This involves being able to learn on their own from their own self-guided exploration, as well as being able to learn from and with others.

Still, scientists are a long way from creating an artificially intelligent robot. After all, if getting a robot to play soccer is so difficult, imagine the challenge involved in getting it to duplicate the capabilities of the human brain!

Cynthia Breazeal posed with one of her inventions—a robotic flower that responds to human touch.

ROBOETHICS

Imagine a future in which artificial intelligence researchers have achieved their goals and robots are as intelligent as human beings. Many ethical issues arise with these new robotic capabilities. If robots are as intelligent as humans, should they still be considered property, or should they now have the same rights as humans? If a robot were to commit a crime, would the robot maker, the robot owner, or the robot itself be held accountable? Are there any kinds of robots that should simply not be created? Will humans lose control of the robots they create?

One of the first people to consider these issues was science fiction author Isaac Asimov. In the 1940s,

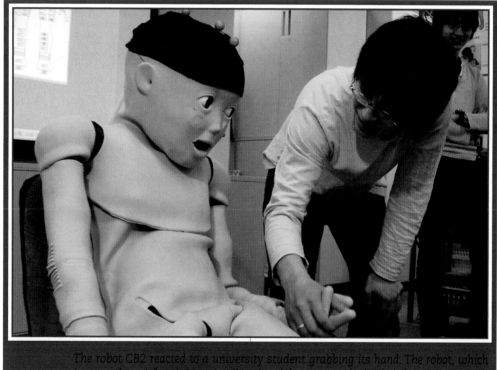

The robot CB2 reacted to a university student grabbing its hand. The robot, which is more than 4 feet (120 cm) tall and weighs 73 pounds (33 kg), has 56 actuators that help it move. It can also speak using an artificial vocal cord.

long before the first personal computer or robotic arm, Asimov was considering these problems in his short stories. In "Runaround," he introduced the Three Laws of Robotics, a set of rules that all robots in his stories must obey. They were:

"First Law: A robot may not injure a human being, or, through inaction, allow a human being to come to harm.

Second Law: A robot must obey orders given [to] it by human beings, except where such orders would conflict with the First Law.

Third Law: A robot must protect its own existence as long as such protection does not conflict with the First or Second Law."

These guidelines address some of the concerns. However, no one knows how to build a robot that will obey. Even still, the laws do not address

The service robots in the movie I, Robot were built to follow the Three Laws of Robotics.

HOAP, Fujitsu's autonomous walking robot, was sold to NASA to help with research in artificial intelligence.

codes of ethics to provide legal guidance for these issues in the future.

AN EXCITING FUTURE

Robots are here to stay. They are so commonplace in manufacturing that industrial robots hardly make the news anymore. Teleoperated robots are common for applications where humans cannot go. But the real excitement involves autonomous robots.

Each year as computers become faster, robots become smarter. Each additional year of AI research offers exciting new capabilities for robots. The next 10 years will bring us many new robots far more capable than those we have today. With this will come great advances for humanity.

issues of the rights of an intelligent man-made machine. The governments of South Korea, Japan, and the European Union are developing robot

It also raises interesting questions we will have to answer about how we will live and work with increasingly intelligent machines. ◤

1495
One of the first recorded designs of a humanoid robot is
created by Leonardo da Vinci

1921
Czech playwright Karel Capek introduces the term *robot* in
his play *R.U.R. (Rossum's Universal Robots)*

1942
Isaac Asimov introduces the Three Laws of Robotics in his
short story "Runaround"

1961
The first industrial robot, the GM Unimate, is installed at a
General Motors assembly plant in New Jersey

1997
The first RoboCup competition is held in Nagoya, Japan

1998
Lego introduces Mindstorms, a set of programmable blocks
that can be used to turn any Lego creation into a robot

2000
The robotic da Vinci Surgical System is introduced,
allowing surgeons to operate remotely and with greater
precision; Honda introduces ASIMO (Advanced Step in
Innovative Mobility), which it calls "the world's most
advanced humanoid robot"

2001
Teleoperated robots from the University of South Florida's
Center for Robot-Assisted Search and Rescue search
the rubble of the World Trade Center for victims of the
September 11 terrorist attacks

2002
Roboticist Cynthia Breazeal of MIT creates Leonardo, a
robot that is designed to learn by interacting with humans

2004
The autonomous robots *Spirit* and *Opportunity* begin
their exploration of Mars; the rovers are still going four
years later

2007
Eleven autonomous robotic vehicles pass the national
qualifying event to compete in the Urban Challenge, a
60-mile (96-km) course that simulates real-life traffic
situations; Carnegie Mellon University and General
Motors' vehicle, named Boss, wins

2008
The *Phoenix* lander reaches Mars after traveling in
space for 10 months; *Phoenix* has a teleoperated
robotic arm that will be used to dig for water
beneath the planet's surface

Timeline

GLOSSARY

actuators
mechanical devices for moving or controlling something

artificial intelligence (AI)
capability of a machine to imitate intelligent human behavior

autonomous
able to act independently

biomimicry
imitating the design of a living thing

humanoid
having human form or characteristics

hydraulic
operated or moved by water or other liquid

lidar
device that measures the distance to an object by bouncing light off the object and timing how long it takes the light to return

manipulators
robotic arms

programs
sequences of computerized instructions

radar
device that measures the distance to an object by bouncing radio waves off the object and timing how long it takes the waves to return

robots
mechanical devices that have a movable body and can take action; often have other components such as a computer and sensors

roboticists
scientists who work in the field of robotics

robotics
field that deals with the design, construction, and operation of robots

sensor fusion
process of combining data from multiple sensors

sensors
devices that receive and respond to stimuli, such as temperature, light, sound, or motion

software
programs used by a computer

sonar
device that measures the distance to an object by bouncing sound waves off the object and timing how long it takes the waves to return

teleoperated
remote-controlled

telerobots
robots that are remotely controlled by a human operator

FURTHER RESOURCES

ON THE WEB

For more information on this topic, use FactHound.

1. Go to *www.facthound.com*
2. Type in this book ID: 0756533775
3. Click on the *Fetch It* button.

FactHound will find the best Web sites for you.

FURTHER READING

Angelo, Joseph A. Jr. *Robot Spacecraft*. New York: Facts on File, 2007.

Domaine, Helena. *Robotics*. Minneapolis: Lerner Publications, 2006.

Jefferis, David. *Robot Workers*. New York: Crabtree Pub. 2007.

Stefoff, Rebecca. *Robots*. Marshall Cavendish Benchmark, 2007.

LOOK FOR OTHER BOOKS IN THIS SERIES:

Climate Crisis: The Science of Global Warming

Cure Quest: The Science of Stem Cell Research

Goodbye, Gasoline: The Science of Fuel Cells

Great Shakes: The Science of Earthquakes

Nature Interrupted: The Science of Environmental Chain Reactions

SOURCE NOTES

Chapter 1: Michael Bay and Matt Ford. "Robots: The Future Is Now." *CNN.com*. 18 April 2006. 29 April 2008. http://edition.cnn.com/2006/TECH/science/04/14/fs.roboticsprofile/

Chapter 2: Mina Kimes. "Need More Workers? Try a Robot." *CNN Money*. 24 Sept. 2007. 29 April 2008. http://money.cnn.com/2007/09/21/smbusiness/Robots.fsb/?postversion=2007092406

Chapter 3: "New Videos Show Predators at Work in Iraq." *CNN.com* February 9 2005. 21 May 2008. www.cnn.com/2005/WORLD/meast/02/08/predator.video/index.html

Chapter 4: Peter Henderson. "No Driver, No Problem as Robot Cars Finish Race." *Reuters*. 3 Nov. 2007. 29 April 2008. www.reuters.com/article/technologyNews/idUSN0245520071103

Chapter 5: Tom Abate. "Public Meeting Will Re-examine Future of Artificial Intelligence." *San Francisco Chronicle*. 7 Sept. 2007. 29 April 2008. www.sfgate.com/cgi-bin/article.cgi?file=/c/a/2007/09/07/MNK8RUU7J.DTL

ABOUT THE AUTHOR

Jennifer Fretland VanVoorst is a writer and editor of books for young people. She enjoys learning about all kinds of scientific and technical topics, from cell biology to computing technology. When she's not reading and writing, VanVoorst enjoys kayaking, playing the harmonica, and watching wildlife. She lives in Minneapolis, Minnesota, with her husband, Brian, and their two wonderful pets.

INDEX